Children's Ministry Guides

Children's Ministry has a commitment to provide the resources and training needed to help busy children's workers develop their ability to evangelise and disciple the children in their community.

Children's Ministry Guides are short, easy-to-read books offering practical insights into key areas of children's ministry. They complement the other resources and training opportunities available from Children's Ministry including:

- conferences
- training days
- distance learning course
- undated, activity-based, Bible-centred teaching programme
- books of ready-to-use ideas
- books of opinion and wisdom from children's ministry practitioners
- CDs and music books of children's praise songs
- supporting resources.

For more details about the Children's Ministry range of resources visit www.childrensministry.co.uk or call 01323 437748.

Other titles in the series:

Tailored
Teaching for 5-9s

SUE PRICE

with
Ruth Alliston, Andy Back,
Jenny Brown, Cathy Kyte

Series edited by Sue Price

CHILDREN'S
MINISTRY

EASTBOURNE

ISBN 1 84291 035 3

Published by
KINGSWAY COMMUNICATIONS LTD
Lottbridge Drove, Eastbourne, BN23 6NT, England.
Email: books@kingsway.co.uk

Book design and production for the publishers by
Bookprint Creative Services, P.O. Box 827, BN21 3YJ, England.
Printed in Great Britain.

For Ruth

my first inspiration to explore
the way that children develop

Contents

Acknowledgements

With hindsight, we can see the way God's plan has worked out in our lives, even when it wasn't clear at the time. As my daughters grew up, I have moved alongside them, becoming involved in toddler group, playgroup, in-school and out-of-school activities. These have brought me into contact with a wide range of wonderful people, who have taught me a great deal about the way that children develop and learn, and I have been provided with a variety of opportunities to observe and interact with children of different ages. At the time, I had no expectation of using the knowledge that I was learning to help train other children's workers.

I would particularly acknowledge Brian Loveridge, who first invited me to become involved in the children's work in our church, and who has continued to encourage me over the years. I would also like to thank the rest of the Children's Ministry team, who support me so effectively.

Sue Price

Introduction

If church is to remain healthy, or even to survive, ministering to children is vital – yet in many churches it is the most under-valued and under-resourced area of ministry.

In a survey conducted in the 1990s, 33 per cent of Christians in the UK said they had found faith by the age of 10. A further 24 per cent found faith between the ages of 11 and 15 (source: *UK Christian Handbook 1999*, Religious Trends section). I can't find any statistics, but anecdotal evidence suggests that Christians who found faith as an adult had generally attended Sunday school or a church-based midweek club as a child, and they could often remember a significant, influencing adult from that period.

By the 1980s, Sunday school attendance was in decline. During the 20 years from 1970 it halved so that, by the end of the 1980s, the percentage of children in church had fallen to 14 per cent, and for 15–19-year-olds the situation was worse, with only 9 per cent attending church. During the 1980s and 1990s, churches began to try and recover this lost generation. Full- or part-time ministers or lay youth workers were appointed to reach out to the over 11s in the community, attempting to attract them back into the church. These youth workers invariably had the under 11s tagged on to their job description, but children's work was not their focus – Sunday school continued under its own steam, operating on the same basis as it had for several previous decades. No one seemed to stop and think: the young people that they were trying to attract had often drifted away from church between the ages 9 and 11. As any marketing manager will tell you, it is easier to retain an existing customer by providing good service than it is to attract a new customer. Primary school aged children love to belong to clubs, and parents welcome holiday clubs and activity days. It should therefore be much easier to attract children, compared with teens, into church activities. If only the children's work was more effective, the task of the youth worker would be so much easier.

This book is about five- to nine-year-olds – helping you to better understand them, and to tailor your teaching to meet their learning needs. If these children enjoy discovering Bible truths and enter willingly into times of prayer and worship, then the church has a vibrant future. A church that is able to minister effectively to their five to nines – helping them discover a head knowledge and, through God's grace, a heart knowledge of Jesus – will have a firm foundation for all its ministry with older children, teens and adults.

Before the age of five

A baby is born totally self-centred; other people are regarded purely as being there to meet their basic needs for food, warmth and love. Gradually, they realise that their carers can help them learn how to meet some of those needs for themselves. They have no reason to question what they are taught – pre-school children will accept everything they are told or shown as right and true. By the time children reach the age of five, they will have experienced about 20 thousand waking hours, and it is said that they have learned half of all they will ever learn. They should certainly have learned to walk and talk and control their bladder, but I don't know how you compare initially learning to walk with continuing to develop your physical skills of ball control to the level of a Premier Division footballer, or how you compare learning to say a few hundred words with developing your mental skills to pass the exams necessary to become a doctor. However, if you work with over-fives, you are not starting with a blank canvas; those 20 thousand hours will have helped shape the way that each child behaves and thinks. It will have provided them with a core of knowledge and opinion.

The impact of millennium culture

We live in a culture defined by rapid advancements in technology. The parents of a five-year-old will have grown up with television, hi-fis, early generation computers and telecommunications. The new generation will grow up with integrated systems based on the Internet, digital TV, and mobile telecommunications. My own children are in their teens and I am as old as the grandmothers of some five-year-olds (just!), but until recently I had felt able to keep pace with advances in technology. Suddenly, I feel unable to keep up with the latest developments. I had understood how computers had downsized from transistors to microchips but now, as they begin to shift from electronic to chemical, their operation shifts beyond my conception. Increasingly I rely on younger generations to provide me with easy-to-use, front-end applications for all the new technology. The new generation don't expect to know all the facts about any subject in this new world – by the time they have learned the information, it could be out of date – and so it becomes more important for them to know how to research current knowledge than to know everything themselves.

Five- to nine-year-old children are also the offspring of a generation of mainly hedonistic consumers. Their parents have grown up in a culture of mass advertising that has aimed, and generally succeeded, to persuade people that increased personal consumption is the best measure of personal happiness, and that increased personal happiness is the ideal to pursue. Children are growing up in a disposable world. Technology advances at a rapid rate, and marketing persuades us that we always need the latest version of everything. Even relationships are not expected to be permanent. What does this mean for those of us who want to convey to children the eternal truth of the Bible and salvation, and the never changing, unconditional love that God has for us?

The teacher's challenge

However excellent the provision that a church makes for children, even if they spent three hours every week in the church environment, that would account for less than 4 per cent of their waking time. Parents and other influential adults, including teachers, will have much more contact time with the children. But parents, even (or perhaps especially) Christian parents, invariably feel ill-equipped to lead their children in the area of spiritual development, and so they abdicate their responsibility to the church. Churches need to consider how they can help parents resume much of their responsibility in this field, after all the Bible charges parents (and grandparents), not the church children's workers, with the task of teaching children.

> Do not forget the things your eyes have seen or let them slip from your heart as long as you live. Teach them to your children and to their children after them. (Deuteronomy 4:9)

> These commandments that I give you today are to be upon your hearts. Impress them on your children. Talk about them when you sit at home and when you walk along the road, when you lie down and when you get up. (Deuteronomy 6:6–7)

However, this book is for the church worker who is sharing the responsibility with the parent, or even acting on the parent's behalf, in teaching children about God, the Bible and salvation. You have the children for such a small proportion of their waking hours; it is vital that you use that time to its very best advantage.

The more you understand about children in general, the greater your responsibility as a teacher becomes. Each child in your group is unique. They are at different stages of development – physically, mentally, emotionally and spiritually – and they prefer to learn in different ways. Each would choose to learn through different activities, and even in different environments. But our natural inclination is to teach in the way that we prefer to learn – we feel happiest offering the activities we enjoy and setting the room out in the way we feel most comfortable. We may even judge the children that we teach as good/bad or bright/less able, depending on how closely they match our own skills and preferences.

As you read this book, you will need to reconsider. Every child in your group is equally important to God. Every one of them needs to have the same opportunity to come to know Jesus as their loving Saviour. Acknowledging that God makes each of us unique, you will be challenged to adjust your teaching to match the development stages and learning preferences of *all* the children in your group. If you are not willing to do that, you are effectively saying that some of the children in your group are less important, or even not important at all, and that you are content to ignore their need for Jesus. While every child is different, the good news is that we can categorise the differences and find ways of constructing sessions that enable every child to learn effectively. And the more you understand about the similarities, and the differences, of the individual children in your teaching group, the easier the task becomes.

Remember that God has called you to minister to children for a purpose. It is a tremendous responsibility and also a tremendous privilege, but it should not be a tremendous burden. If, as you read this book, you ask God for his guidance on its application to your situation, you can be confident that he will be with you as you plan and as you teach.

The chapters in this book are divided into two parts. The first part will help you understand and categorise the developmental stages and learning preferences of the children with whom you work who are between five- and nine-years-old. The second part will give you strategies and ideas for tailoring your teaching to best serve those children in their walk with God.

Sue Price

Part One
Understanding Children

Nothing can help you understand children better than observation and conversation. Watch them interact, discover what they talk about, what they enjoy doing together and individually, which games they like to play, which TV programmes they enjoy, which stories they like, the kind of music they listen to. . . The following chapters include thumbnail sketches of five typical children. As you read about Serena, Josh, Natalie, Tom and Melissa, compare and contrast their characteristics with those of the children you know.

The two chapters in this section will give you a context for your observations. The first gives typical stages of physical, social and emotional, mental, and spiritual development for children between the ages of five and nine. Development from birth to and through adulthood is, of course, a continuous process, and does not happen in discreet steps at certain, pre-determined ages, but knowing the expectations for 'average' children will help you understand the individuals in your group, and help you see the uniqueness of each one! The second chapter outlines the wide diversity of ways in which children prefer to learn.

Part One
Understanding Children

1. The Growing Child

This chapter is a practical guide that explores the typical behaviour and development levels for five- to nine-year-old children. Of course, no child is absolutely typical in every area, and you will know children who differ widely from the developmental stages given below. However, by knowing the typical behaviour and abilities of children of different ages, you can plan sessions more effectively, and you can understand where it might be necessary to modify pre-prepared materials if your own children are struggling to achieve, or are well ahead of the average. Much of this chapter summarises the practical conclusions drawn from conducted detailed research and studies carried out over the last 50 years. Many of these studies have been written from a secular viewpoint but, if you wish to spend more time reading some of the detailed research and resultant theories, James Fowler's book *Stages of Faith* (HarperCollins, 1995) sets out his own ideas and those of Kohlberg, Eriksson and Piaget in a readable manner. Westerhoff has recently reviewed and updated his own book *Will Our Children Have Faith?* (Morehouse Publishing, 2000).

Physical development

Enormous physical changes will have taken place between birth and the age of five – children are standing upright and are mobile. From five to nine years the changes will be less dramatic, but there is still a lot going on. Children grow taller and heavier and learn new physical skills.

It may seem to be stating the obvious, but a five-year-old child is still small! Typically around 108 cm (3 ft 6 ins) tall, they are only about 60 per cent of their projected adult height. Over the next four years, they will grow less rapidly than either earlier in infancy or later in puberty – approximately 5–6 cm (2½ ins) per year – so that by nine years old they will have grown to 130–135 cm (4 ft 3 ins –

CASE STUDY

Serena is five years old and 106 cm tall. She loves to dance, and wants to show off her dancing to any adult who is willing to watch. She likes to talk to those adults too – telling them all about her dancing in detail! When she's at her dancing class, she wants to help her teacher by showing the rest of the class what to do and pointing out when they do things wrong. She is not generally very interested in sitting and doing things – she is just beginning to read and write, and she sometimes spends time painting, enjoying the different colours and shapes she can make on the paper – but she does always enjoy sitting and listening to the stories that her grandma makes up for her, especially when she can help grandma remember the ending of a story that she told a few days previously. Serena has always gone to church with her family, and she knows that Jesus loves her always. She talks to him just like she talks to any other adult that will listen!

4 ft 5 ins). Go into schools and see the furniture used in the children's classrooms. Tables and chairs are tailored to the size of the children; there is not an expectation – so often made in church halls – that one size (adult size, of course!) fits all. Imagine how frustrating it is to have to climb on and off chairs that are too high and leave your legs dangling, and then to have to use a table that forces your arms and hands to be in unnaturally high positions above your shoulders!

Between the ages of five and nine, children are mastering new motor skills. By five they can usually run, jump, hop, walk up and down stairs, catch a ball and hold a knife and fork. Over the next four years, they will be learning new skills, such as using a bat to hit a ball, skip, swim using recognisable strokes, skate and ride a bike. At the younger end of the age range, the children will be restless and constantly eager to 'have a go', but will easily be distracted by an alternative activity and will tire rapidly. Showing you how fast they can run, how high they can jump, or how accurately they can kick a ball will be important. Older children will have greater staying power and may be very persistent in practising new, complex physical skills. Eight- and nine-year-olds will usually enjoy organised team games, but they are likely to become boisterous – so clear the playing area and be prepared for minor accidents!

Finer skills and hand–eye co-ordination will also be developing. Five-year-olds will still be clumsy in the way they use pencils and paint brushes, and will need considerable help with activities that require cutting or detailed manipulation of craft materials. By nine they will be much more dexterous. For some this will mean that they can dash off a drawing or craft with increasing speed, ready to move onto the next activity as quickly as possible, while for others it will mean that they can persevere, getting every last detail of their picture or craft right. Improving pencil skills also means an improved writing ability. Writing is linked closely to linguistic skills, but a five-year-old will only just have the motor skills required to write large letters and single words, such as their name or simple nouns. By nine the disparity in writing skills between children will be quite marked. Some will be struggling to form readable sentences, while others will be writing fluent paragraphs of neat text.

For five-year-olds the world is still very tangible – they can learn so much more about an object if they touch it or pick it up. By nine they have improved observational skills, and can make judgements about things without always having to touch them, and this increased awareness also shows in their art. At five, all the people a child draws will stand face on and look straight out of the paper at you. By eight or nine, they will begin to introduce perspective to their pictures, people and animals will have more realistic body proportions and may be drawn in action.

Social and emotional development

Babies are at the mercy of their own needs, and other people are regarded as being around purely to service those needs. Toddlers are not quite so dependent on others but remain essentially selfish, not understanding the possibility of other people having needs that conflict with their own.

By five, children are beginning to see themselves as

individuals who fit into a structure of relationships with family, friends and other influential adults. They are starting to recognise the rights of others, but self-constraint and consideration only comes gradually – firstly to please parents and other significant carers, and later because they realise that it helps them to be accepted and liked by their peers.

They are just starting to understand what the nouns mother, father, aunt, uncle, brother and sister signify and, as they understand, they become loyal to and show pride in their family. With siblings, especially younger brothers and sisters, this new understanding of relationship may manifest itself in bossiness, protectiveness, jealousy or even violence!

CASE STUDY

Josh is six years old and 114 cm tall. He's very active most of the time, swimming, just riding his bike without stabilisers, and wanting to learn to roller-skate. But he will also spend considerable periods of time with toys that he can build, sort, order and count – he has just learned to count large numbers, and knows that he has 653 Lego bricks. He likes spending time with his great-grandad in his shed, sorting out screws and things, and listening to stories about Grandad and Daddy when they were boys. He has three friends in his class – George, Lucy and Adam – and he likes to tell them all about his family – his sisters, his aunts, his uncles, his grannies and grandads and his great-grandad. He knows he has got five cousins, and he can name them all. Josh goes to church with his grandparents. He has only been going for a year – since Granny and Grandad moved to live close by. When it is Granny's turn to make the coffee after a service, he likes to help by passing the biscuits round to everyone.

Young children will begin to make friends with children of the same age, although they are still self-centred, and find the necessary give and take of friendships hard to sustain. This self-centredness also means that they want to be the focus of attention and will often try and dominate social situations by showing off or being naughty. They are still looking to adults for approval and encouragement, and yet at the same time want to assert their own will and may be rude or defiant. These first steps to forming relationships with others of their own age will be much easier for children who have experienced love and acceptance and have a good self-image. Those who have suffered tension and criticism at home will be anxious and defensive and are likely to find it much harder to make friends.

As children get older, by seven or eight, having a best friend becomes very important. This is especially true for girls – boys are often happy to remain in looser friendship groups. Spending time with their peers becomes more attractive than spending time with family or other adults, and they begin to learn to subordinate their own wants to those of the group, and start to develop social skills.

By eight or nine, children will have developed their understanding of family relationships into a wider understanding of their community, and will be aware of their racial and ethnic backgrounds. They will be beginning to seek a degree of independence from parental domination, and older children or teens may form their role models. Loosely formed 'clubs' will often dominate their social time and these peer groupings will usually be single-sex, as a growing hostility develops between boys and girls.

Five-year-olds need to succeed – they want to win games, to quickly master a new skill, to gain an adult's attention. They easily become frustrated and annoyed by their own failure, and tears and tantrums are likely to be the result. They need constant encouragement and a sense of a secure environment, in terms of familiar surroundings and a routine, to be able to continually push the boundaries and develop new skills.

As they get older, tantrums are likely to be replaced by fits of sulking, and emotions will swing back and forth. They are ready to tackle most new challenges, and will get excited and fired up by them, but quickly despondent and uninterested if they don't immediately succeed.

Five- to seven-year olds will often respond negatively to direct demands; they will be much more positive to indirect reminders and guidance. By eight, children will begin to develop self-discipline responding to peer group responsibilities.

Younger children, wanting to show that they know what is 'right', will be critical of other children's behaviour, and will be quick to tell the adults in charge when someone else is 'wrong'. As they get older, children begin to empathise with others and will give and take peer criticism, being in less of a hurry to take grievances to adults. Between the ages of five and nine, children shift from seeing adults as the owners of all knowledge and the solvers of all problems, to realising that they may be fallible and may not have the solutions to every problem. At the same time (and possibly as a consequence) children begin to develop fears that they no longer share with adults – fears of the dark, of animals, of not having friends, of failure at school or in other areas.

Mental development

Five-year-olds think in very concrete terms. Show them a marble and a tennis ball and they will tell you the tennis ball is bigger. Show them a tennis ball and a football and they will tell you the football is bigger. Take the balls away and ask them which is bigger, the marble or the football, and they will ask to see the two together. By eight or nine, they will be able to make the comparison by imagination, and will no longer need to see the marble and the football again. This is the beginning of abstract thought, although the link to physical, or concrete, objects is still required.

CASE STUDY

Natalie is seven years old and 120 cm tall. She likes swimming, but is quite clumsy when it comes to other activities, and hasn't managed to learn to ride a bike yet. She likes drama, and relates well to others – both adults and children. She and her best friend, Hannah, will often organise others in the class to write and perform a short play for their teacher. When the others don't take it as seriously as Natalie, she is inclined to go off in a huff, but it never lasts long – Hannah tells her a joke and it's all forgotten. Natalie is dyslexic, and is struggling to learn to read and spell, so she is really pleased when her mum or dad spend time reading her fantasy stories – especially the C.S. Lewis Narnia *books. She is keen to draw and paint and do other craft activities, but if she finds them hard she will leave them unfinished. Natalie has always gone to church with Mum (Dad and her brother usually stay at home), and she often prays to God about things that are happening, confident that God listens and cares about her very much.*

At five, a child can recognise a simple sequence. Gradually, children begin to observe patterns and make comparisons between objects, enabling them to group things into categories. However, before the age of seven or eight, children do not understand the concepts and sequencing of distance, time and money – recall all those journeys with younger children where, no matter how many times you have explained that the trip will take three hours, as it is 100 miles to your destination, the question, 'Are we nearly there yet?' is asked incessantly after the first 15 minutes. Eventually, the ability to categorise and sequence items develops, and knowledge about one object can be transferred to a new object if it has the same feature – for instance, a nine-year-old will realise that anything with a lead and a plug on the end has to be connected, via a socket, to electricity, to make it work.

This age group learns best by active participation. Their attention span is increasing – typically from about 5–10 minutes at five to 10–15 minutes at nine – but this average will vary enormously according to the activity and the interest it holds for the individual child. Younger children will be eager to learn, but will often get discouraged and move onto a new activity, while older children will have more persistence and be less likely to give up if tasks are initially difficult. Five-year-olds will remember facts that are presented in a context that is relevant to themselves – if it is something they experience, such as all the details about a vet's visit with a new puppy, or can observe, such as a detailed description of the colour and make of Grandad's new car. By eight or nine, they are curious about everything, and will have a voracious appetite for new information about almost anything.

Five to nines enjoy stories, especially when there is lots of action and adventure, and they will now differentiate between reality and fantasy. Almost all children in the age range will appreciate having stories read to them, and older children, who do not have specific reading difficulties, will enjoy reading to themselves. Joke books and comics will be particularly popular with many.

Art is an excellent way for children to express themselves, particularly for younger children, who have less developed writing and language skills. However, be prepared for five-year-olds to completely change the title and context of a picture if you ask them about it some time after it was initially drawn. It was created in one context, but looking at it again may spark a new train of thought in their mind. Use children's art work as a way of initiating conversation, but don't correct or criticise their masterpiece!

Vocabulary develops alongside other mental skills. Five-year-olds talk mainly about things, rather than feelings. If they are describing someone, they will look at their visible features. 'Nice' or 'nasty' is about as far as they will go in describing character. By seven or eight, looks, rather than behaviour, will usually determine their opinion of a person's character. Their judgement also tends to be extreme – people are awful or wonderful and 'very' is a well-used word. Later, children will begin to realise that people are not generally so clear-cut, and that an individual's behaviour can vary between good and bad, but only a few nine-year-olds will have reached this level of discernment.

Five-year-olds begin to develop the ability to know right from wrong, although self-restraint only comes gradually, and a child who is considerate one minute may be very selfish again the next. At five or six, their decision as to whether something is classified as 'right' or 'wrong' is usually determined by the reaction of adults to the particular behaviour. Even in matters of safety, the child's decision to avoid running out into the road will be based on the fact that the action will be met with disapproval, rather than self-preservation. As they get older, moral reasoning becomes more determined by a need to be accepted by peers and, eventually, personal feelings of fairness. Eight- and nine-year-olds become very sensitive to justice and fair play.

CASE STUDY

Tom is eight years old and 130 cm tall. He loves football, and any other rough-and-tumble, team or group game that he can persuade one of his friends, especially Billy or Joel, to play with him. They all support the local team, and love it when one of their dads takes them to a match. He likes to be around people, and he loves telling everyone his latest joke, so he isn't very interested in solitary activities – he will dash off writing, drawing or crafts as quickly as possible to move onto something else. He is quite musical, though, and is happy to sing in the choir because Joel goes, too. He would like to learn to play the drums and thinks that, if he doesn't become a football star, he and Billy and Joel could form a band! He won't admit to anyone, especially his friends, that he is sometimes afraid if he wakes up in the night and it is very dark. He tries to remember to pull the curtain back before he goes to sleep, so that the light from the street lamp shines into his room. Tom has always gone to church with his family. He was sure that God loved him, but now he is beginning to hear boys at school saying that church is 'sissy', and he sometimes wonders if God is really there at all.

Spiritual and faith development

Children as young as five, or even younger, may make declarations of faith, accepting that Jesus died to take the blame for the things they do wrong. We know from the Bible that God uses children of all ages (consider Samuel, 1 Samuel 3 and Joash, 2 Chronicles 23–24) and the Holy Spirit can work in the lives of young children today. However, as children grow and develop mentally, they will need to expand their spiritual understanding and re-examine their commitment. Some will seamlessly move through childhood, readjusting their understanding of salvation, and eventually coming to a strong, personal commitment to Christ in their teens. Others may falter and even drift away from an early commitment. Other children may hear and learn about Jesus from an early age, but may not make a commitment of faith until they are adults, or may never make a commitment at all. Yet others may not hear about Jesus until they are older. This begs the question of someone ministering to five to nines – are they an evangelist or a pastor?

Children's spiritual development is in some ways closely tied to their mental development. What can five-year-olds understand about God? They can know him as the Creator of all the things they see. They can understand that Jesus, and other Bible characters, were real people. They can have a simple understanding of sin, knowing that we can choose to do right things or wrong things. And they can have a basic awareness that Jesus took the blame for all the wrong things that we do, died, came alive again, and will return to earth again one day. Five-year-olds can also pray – they will model patterns of prayer that they see and will be far less self-conscious in group prayer than will older children.

As we have already discovered, children under the age of five have no ability to distinguish between fact and fantasy. They will regard any stories they have been told about Jesus, any facts about God as true without question. From five upwards, children are beginning to understand that some of the stories they have heard as younger children, for instance Father Christmas or Cinderella, are fantasy and it is important that they don't begin to put God in the same category. They may begin to ask questions about who made God and where is God, but remember their level of mental development is such that they cannot cope with long, theological replies, and they will accept that you may not know all the answers yourself – being honest is most important.

By seven or eight, children are looking for information in every area, and they will have an active interest in finding out more about God and Jesus. They can understand that Jesus is God's Son, and as they grasp the concept of time they can start to put Bible stories into sequence and begin to understand the relationship between the Old and New Testaments. As reading skills develop, they can start to look up verses and read passages for themselves. Their strict sense of fairness will often lead them to question why God let Jesus die for the wrong things that everyone else does.

By nine years old, children may be discerning right from wrong by their own conscience, rather than on the say so of adults. They will want to be good, and will feel shame when they do wrong. They will also be seeing that adults can't always solve every problem for them and answer every question they have, and so they will start to realise that they have a need for an omnipotent God. They may well be ready to accept Christ as their personal Saviour.

A child's development is a natural progression, dependent on growth, brain development and nurture. Their physical, emotional, social and mental growth starts at birth and, unless they have specific disabilities or suffer from severe lack of nurture, they will all pass through the same stages of development at roughly the same age. This means that we can know the key characteristics of typical five-, six-, seven-, eight- and nine-year-olds.

CASE STUDY

Melissa is nine years old. She is a good reader and enjoys reading books, especially stories about animals, and spends a lot of time on her own, or with her best friend, Jess, drawing and colouring, writing stories, or playing imaginative games – usually where they are vets. They hate boys, and all their boisterous games, but enjoy going to Brownies. They are about to go on Pack Holiday and she is excited, but a little apprehensive, about going away without her parents for the first time. She has found out everything she can about the village they are staying in, and the local town that Brown Owl has plans to visit, but she is worried that she might not be very good at some of the more adventurous activities, and she doesn't want to be made fun of by the other Brownies. She plays the recorder, and is about to start piano lessons. Melissa only started going to church after she became a Brownie, at seven. Her family doesn't go, but she asked if she could attend with Jess after going to several special services with the Brownies. She is keen to learn about Jesus, but she isn't sure that she would call herself a Christian – she thinks it was a bit mean of God to let Jesus die on the cross for something he didn't even do.

Faith development is not so easily defined. Children may not grow up in a family where faith is acknowledged or where God is mentioned, except as a swear word. They may come to your church club at eight years old, having no idea who Jesus is, or what prayer means. However, we know that faith does progress:

> Like newborn babies, crave pure spiritual milk, so that by it you may grow up in your salvation, now that you have tasted that the Lord is good. (1 Peter 2:2–3)

We can look at faith development as a pilgrimage where we all have a path to travel and where, at some point along that path, by God's grace, we can meet him personally. There are some similarities with the progression through the other stages of physical and mental development that we have explored. Recall the terrible pictures from the 1980s of infants and children in Romanian orphanages. They showed the results of an extreme lack of physical, social, emotional and mental nurture. However, happier images were shown over the next few years, as these children began to develop in all areas once they were shown love and provided with basic care and education.

The children that you minister to may have experienced faith at home and in the church community since birth, or they may be coming to you completely deprived of faith nurturing. With the first group, you will be helping them along their pathway of faith, recognising that, even with this group, some will have travelled further and explored more deeply than others. With the second group, you will need to provide basic input about Jesus and God's love for them, enabling them to start out on their own journey of faith.

Summary

Some of the key characteristics from the chapter are tabulated below:

Typically, at five years old, a child:	*Typically, by nine years old, a child:*
Physically	
• is about 108 cm tall	• is about 130–135 cm tall
• can run, jump, hop, climb stairs	• can skip, swim, skate, ride a bike
• can catch a ball	• can hit a ball with a bat
• is clumsy in their use of pens, scissors etc.	• is more dexterous
• is beginning to write words	• may be a fluent, neat writer
• is eager to try new skills	• is persistent in skill practice
Socially and emotionally	
• finds friendships hard to sustain	• has best friends
• wants to be the focus of attention	• will put group needs first
• wants adult approval	• wants peer approval
• understands 'family'	• understands 'community'
• has tantrums	• sulks
Mentally	
• thinks in concrete terms	• begins to think in abstract
• understands simple sequences	• understands time, distance, money
• determines right/wrong by reactions	• has concepts of fair play and justice
Spiritually	
can understand:	can understand:
• God as Creator	• a need for an omnipotent God
• Jesus as a real person	• Jesus is God's Son
• prayer	• the sequence of the Bible
• the choice between right and wrong	• a feeling of shame when they do wrong

2. Learning Preferences

The previous chapter looked at the way that children develop physically, socially, emotionally, mentally and spiritually between the ages of five and nine. They are constantly learning new skills and information, but the way that they learn and the circumstances under which they learn most effectively will not be the same for all children. Each one of us has a preferred way of learning, some elements varying with age, and other elements remaining fixed throughout our lives.

God made each one of us unique – just as we all have distinctive fingerprints, so we have distinctive ways of learning. But just as fingerprints can be categorised by whorls and other patterns, so our learning preferences can be broken into groups and categories. Much of the following draws from the work of Marlene LeFever, *Learning Styles: Reaching everyone God gave you to teach* (Kingsway Publications, 1998). If you wish to explore aspects of this chapter in greater depth I would recommend *Learning Styles* as a very readable book.

Preferred senses

We receive information through all of our senses and, generally, the more senses we involve in any learning experience the better we will retain the information. However, we each have sensory preferences for learning and, if we are not given the opportunity to bring those senses into use, we will tend to 'switch off', and will be far less likely to learn effectively.

Watch a baby begin to make sense of a new object. If she is able, she will pick up the object and put it to, or in, her mouth. Her tongue and lips are sensitive receptors, her nose is close by, and she wants to be able to experience the object – what it feels, tastes and smells like. Toddlers are into everything – the way they learn best is by touch and activity. This method of learning is known as tactile/kinesthetic, or T/K for short, and all pre-school children can be described as having a T/K sensory preference for learning. Many people, especially boys and men, retain a T/K preference for learning right through adulthood – wanting to learn through experience, and needing to move around, constantly shifting in their chair if they are forced to remain seated.

CASE STUDY

Serena is an imaginative learner. She is always happy to talk about her own experiences to the teacher and the rest of her group – especially if she can tell them about her dancing! At five, she still prefers to learn in a T/K way, and will generally be found talking to herself while she is playing make-believe games with either other children or her toys.

Between the ages of five and nine, some children shift to a visual learning preference, and by nine years old it will be the preference of the majority of children. They lose the need to move around, and will find that the stimuli of pictures, diagrams and words are their best aids for effective learning. These children will want a pencil in their hand – drawing, doodling or (as they get older) note taking – as they are taught. Again, many people retain a visual preference for learning through adulthood.

Around, or after, the age of eleven, some youngsters will shift to an auditory learning preference, remembering most effectively what they hear (words, music and other sounds). None of the children in the age range covered by this book will have an auditory learning preference, but we will need to take it into account later, when we examine the effect of the teacher's learning preferences on the children being taught.

The apostle John may have been the first to record the importance of involving different senses in learning:

> That which was from the beginning, which we have <u>heard</u>, which we have <u>seen</u> with our eyes, which we have looked at and our hands have <u>touched</u> – this we proclaim concerning the Word of life. (1 John 1:1 – my underlining)

As was noted at the beginning of this section, the more senses we involve in learning, the more effective the process is. Whether they have a T/K or visual preference, all five- to nine-year-olds need the opportunity to see (an object, visual aid, picture or video), talk about and, if possible, interact with new information, or practise a new skill.

Preferred environment

You may criticise the room or hall that you teach in because it is dingy, needs decorating, is too cramped, or doesn't have very appropriate furniture. But you probably don't consider that, without you changing the content of your session or your teaching methods in any way, the room that you are using can significantly affect the amount of the session that the children connect with or learn. Factors such as lighting levels, temperature, background noise and room layout will all influence learning – and, as we don't all have the same preferences, you will be seeking compromise in many cases.

Young children often find bright light a problem. The ultraviolet rays emitted from fluorescent lighting, in particular, can lead to headaches, or just a general feeling of malaise, so that children are unreceptive. Contrary to what we might expect, poor readers will generally read better at low lighting levels. As we get older, we need more light – you, the teacher, will naturally feel more comfortable with more lighting than the children require.

Background sound can also have an impact on learning. You will hear some children humming, or singing, or even

CASE STUDY

Josh is mainly a common-sense learner, but he does show analytic characteristics as well. He is still a T/K learner, too. He likes to try everything out for himself, and is very hands-on. He always enjoys games and activities that involve moving around, but is happy to sit, preferably on the floor, as long as he has something to do (likes bricks to build with or a car to push around).

talking quietly to themselves. These children learn better when there is background noise. Others prefer quiet or silence. Similarly, temperature, either too hot or too cold, will influence learning – and we don't all have the same preference.

Room design and layout affect how receptive we are to teaching. Where do you sit to prepare your sessions? Do you sit or sprawl on a sofa, or comfortable chair, sit propped up in bed, or sit on an upright chair at a table? Children are no different – many find that a more casual setting is more enjoyable and conducive to learning. Giving them an option to sit on beanbags, or even sprawl on the floor, can improve learning by up to 20 per cent.

These are all environmental factors that you should be able to influence, to at least some degree. A fifth environmental factor is the time of the session. A few five to nines, generally creative types (excelling at art, dance, sport or music), prefer to perform and learn during late afternoon or evening. Just under 30 per cent are 'early morning' people, who perform and learn best first thing in the day, but the majority of this age group are at their peak between 10am and 2pm. A final factor, which I have classified as environmental as it doesn't readily fit elsewhere, is that some children seem to have improved focus when they are chewing or eating.

Research has shown that children with diverse special needs tend to perform best in environments that have low lighting, a warm temperature, background sound and an informal room layout.

Preferred styles

Some of the children in your group will always want to be
talking, and others will be fiddling with any craft materials
on the table before you ever want them to. Yet others will
be coming up with crazy suggestions as to what you
should do during today's session, while the remainder will
be sitting waiting for you to start, and getting annoyed that
you haven't yet told them what today's story is going to be
about.

Such children are showing the characteristics of the four
categories of learning styles. We don't all fit neatly into one
category, but most people have one, or possibly two, domi-
nant styles, and these traits apply throughout our lives –
from childhood through adulthood.

The children who always want to talk are classified as
'imaginative' learners. They learn best by interacting with
others. They like sharing and building on other people's
ideas, and would much rather work in groups than individually. They are people-centred, caring about the impact
of events on the characters in a story, but the details of the

CASE STUDY

*Natalie is a dynamic learner. She is full of ideas, and is always
trying to organise the rest of her group into carrying them out.
Although she has problems with reading, she is showing signs of
being a visual learner and a developing artist, constantly drawing plans for her latest project – although she rarely finishes a
plan because she has already moved on to the next idea! She often
complains that she has a headache when she is in a room with
fluorescent lighting.*

story are rarely seen as important – only the broad sweep and its implications. They will want to understand the relevance of a session to their own lives before they see any point in taking part in the lesson. They will often pull the whole group together, but they can be disruptive by monopolising conversations and refusing to stop talking. These children generally like background noise and a setting with plenty of colour. They are 'Can I tell you what happened to me when . . . ?' children, and they are particularly attracted to faith because of the love available through Christ.

The children who want to be 'hands-on' are classified as 'common-sense' learners. They are active, often with a T/K sensory preference, and practical. They have an idea, or are told something, and they want to try it for themselves. If something works one way, then they want to experiment – to see what happens when they change some of the variables. Common-sense learners are logical, and they need to see the relevance of learning – they don't enjoy reading, unless it is an instruction or guide book. They will be determined to make projects succeed, but this can become negative if they start to dominate other children to try and achieve a deadline. These children generally like background noise and the opportunity to move around as they learn. They are 'What happens if I press this button?' children, and they want others to see their faith validated by service.

The children with crazy ideas are classified as 'dynamic' learners. They love to stand out in the group – they want to be different, they can make others laugh, and their enthusiasm often causes them to become the natural leaders of the group, but they often don't have organisational abilities, and are not necessarily the ones you would choose to lead! They are rarely interested in detail, and will guess answers rather than 'waste' time looking them up, but they will come up with creative ideas, particularly regarding the application of a story to your own surroundings. They can make intuitive judgements and decisions, but they can also be egotistic, manipulating others and refusing to recognise their contribution. These children generally like to learn in a setting that they have had the opportunity to influence. They are 'But why don't we do *this* instead?' children, and they tend to be intuitive believers.

Finally, the children who fit the description of the ideal scholar – those who sit quietly and wait to be given all the facts. These children are classified as 'analytic' learners. They prefer to work alone, and need to know if they are 'right' or 'wrong' – they would much rather sit and watch than join in open-ended discussion or role-play activities. They want to know what the 'expert' says (that may be the Bible, another book, the Internet, or you) and they get very

CASE STUDY

Tom sometimes seems to be an imaginative learner, and at other times displays common-sense characteristics. He is still a T/K learner, and shows every sign of remaining that way! He never likes to be still, and if he is expected to sit and listen or watch you will notice him wriggling in his seat, beating out a rhythm on his imaginary drum set, and humming a tune, or chatting to the boy sitting next to him. He often complains he is too hot, even though he is usually only wearing his favourite football shirt.

frustrated if you run out of time and they can't finish a story or an activity. They are focused on knowledge rather than people, and they may be intolerant of others in the group if they don't show a similar commitment to learning. These children generally prefer a formal and quiet setting. They are 'Please tell me, have I have done this right?' children, and they will weigh all sides of the Christianity issue, reading the Bible and making sure that what Christ offers makes sense, before they are willing to move forward in faith.

Impact of teacher's preferences

The foregoing sections tell us that we each have preferred ways of learning and, when we assume the role of teacher, our natural inclination is to teach in the way we like to learn. If it is within our control, we will set the room in the way we find most conducive for learning, and we will teach in the way that matches our learning style, environment and sensory preferences. This is excellent news for the children that learn in the same way as their teacher, and disastrous news for the rest.

What would happen to our five children, Serena, Josh, Natalie, Tom and Melissa, if they found themselves in a group being taught by an auditory, analytic learner who had not been given the help or skills to teach in any other way? Although our teacher is an auditory learner, she does not think the lesson is a time for general conversation. She will ask Serena to stop chattering away and to tell her about her dancing class later, after the lesson, and she will ask the children to sit down quietly so that she can introduce the topic of the lesson. The lesson is about Moses and the Israelites in the desert: well that's all right – all the children enjoy a good story, and the teacher has done her preparation and can tell it in appropriate language, without a book. But she hasn't thought to provide any pictures or other visual aids and, after a couple of minutes, Serena wanders away from the table and has to be called back. Tom then turns to Josh, makes a comment about how his mum wouldn't like having to eat the same thing every day – she is always complaining that he only ever wants to eat pizza and chips – and he has to be hushed. Natalie opens the box of pens on the table, and starts to draw on a sheet of paper. Tom helps himself to a pen and starts to tap the edge of the table, and then Josh takes a handful of pens and starts sorting them into colours. Melissa is the only one to concentrate on the story to the end. Now the teacher wants to talk about the point of the story – what the children can learn that applies to their own lives. Serena and the boys have had enough of sitting, and are no longer interested in talking about a story that doesn't seem to have any relevance to them – after all, they don't wander around a desert, and Mum can pop into Tesco whenever they need food. Melissa is happy to retell the story, but can't make a connection to herself, either. Natalie has a

CASE STUDY

Melissa is a classic analytical learner. She would much rather be sitting at a table reading, writing or drawing by herself than joining in group activities and she often complains that the others in the group are making too much noise. She is very much a visual learner, seeking out information from reference books and the Internet.

brilliant idea – why don't they all eat only cereal for a week, and give the money they save to the missionary family they support in Africa? (Natalie is quite sure there's a desert in Africa.) But the teacher doesn't really think it's a good idea, and she brings the lesson to a close. She goes home knowing that she told the story well, but wishing that she had children who were less disruptive.

Hopefully, this is not the pattern of most children's groups and activities in church – but it may not be far removed from much of what happens in the church services that children attend. There is not generally an opportunity to move around, or to discuss your own experiences and work out how they fit with the Bible passage being studied. Visual aids may be used during the talk but rarely in prayer times or during the singing (except song sheets that young children can't read anyway). And no one is allowed to throw in random ideas during the talk, or invited to suggest a way of living the sermon out during the coming week in school, or at the workplace, or at home.

Does this chapter help us understand why children (and some adults) find church services boring or difficult?

Part Two
Tailored Teaching

The first section of this book has sought to help you better understand the five to nines that you minister to. Although each is unique, we can learn about typical stages of child development and learning preferences, and ensure that we prepare sessions that take these into account. This way, we can give every child an equal opportunity to come to know Jesus as their loving Saviour.

Remember that you are not called to do this alone and in your own strength. Paul knew that as he travelled, teaching about Jesus, he was dependent on God's Spirit to convict people of Christ's saving grace.

> You show that you are a letter from Christ, the result of our ministry, written not with ink but with the Spirit of the living God, not on tablets of stone but on tablets of human hearts.
>
> Such confidence as this is ours through Christ before God. Not that we are competent in ourselves to claim anything for ourselves, but our competence comes from God. He has made us competent as ministers of a new covenant. (2 Corinthians 3:3–6a)

You, the teacher, are a bridge. You provide a channel for information, enabling the taught to discover or learn new truths. As someone who works in the area of children's ministry, you have the most exciting learning aim of all – the ultimate desire is to see a change in children as they accept Christ's message of salvation and apply it to their own lives. You may be the bridge, but the Holy Spirit is present as your support. You can provide facts about Jesus, but the Holy Spirit will bring children to a faith in Jesus. You can demonstrate and teach about a Christian lifestyle, but the Holy Spirit will convict the children to want to adopt it as their own. You can give head knowledge, but only the Holy Spirit will give heart knowledge.

But, however much we recognise the role of God in our teaching, we should not forget that he provides us with training opportunities so that we can perform the task he has given us to the best of our ability. We know that God can heal, but that doesn't stop us investing considerable sums of money in training doctors and nurses and in medical research. By the same token, God has called us to teach children, and we must use and develop our skills to honour him. Understanding children should enable us to be more effective channels for the truth of salvation.

This section of the book has two chapters that look at the teaching environment and a cycle of learning that meets the needs of all learners. It then concludes with two chapters that look at some specific learning activities, and sample sessions that are appropriate for five- to nine-year-olds.

- You can provide facts about Jesus; the Holy Spirit will bring children to a faith in Jesus.
- You can demonstrate and teach about a Christian lifestyle; the Holy Spirit will convict the children to want to adopt it as their own.
- You can give head knowledge; the Holy Spirit will give heart knowledge.

3. The Teaching Environment

Your room: Lights! Curtain! Action!

With this age group, it's lights (no thanks), curtain (probably left closed), and action (yes please, definitely!).

You may have read the section on preferred environment and thought, 'Well, that's all very well, but it's impossible to do anything about the church hall (or school classroom that we only hire on Sunday) that I have to teach in.' Some factors will be beyond your control, but there are still things you can do.

It will not be easy to change the time you meet, as most Sunday sessions will be timed to fit in with the main worship service, and for mid-week clubs you will be constrained to meet out-of-school hours. However, most churches will have their Sunday worship during the period that hits the most receptive time for the majority of five to nines – between 10 am and 2 pm.

What about the decoration of the room you meet in? I travel around the country a fair bit, using church and school facilities for training events. Recently, while looking at potential venues for a training day, we visited two schools. They were in the same town and served similar communities with, I suspect, many of the children at both entitled to free school lunches. As we toured the first school with the site manager, he apologised for the poor state of decoration, saying that they had to spend most of their building budget just repairing the damage caused by the children. We saw evidence of this as we walked round, with maintenance staff mending the hinges of a door, and the site manager needing to use his phone on a couple of occasions to notify them of a new piece of damage. There was graffiti on the walls, and children were out in the play-ground, riding bikes and chatting, and this during lesson time. What was also noticeable was the air of neglect in the classrooms – with damaged furniture, missing doors and little effort to display children's work – and that the notice-boards in corridors and communal areas were generally in a terrible state, with out-of-date notices, untidily written and half torn off, or no notices at all. We spoke to no one other than the site manager, so I can't say whether there were specific problems and reasons for the particular state of disrepair, but it was clear that at least some of the children were responding to the neglect of the building through their own behaviour.

Going through the doors of the second school that morning was a very different story. There were showcases of children's work in the corridors, the notice-boards had well presented, up-to-date notices, the classrooms were tidy, with interesting displays on the walls, and they even had carpets! The caretaker commented that there was a policy of removing graffiti as soon as it appeared – he said that out of sight, out of mind meant that it rarely reappeared – and there were no children wandering around aimlessly. The whole school had a feeling of industry and pride in itself. It was clear that, by investing in the environment, the children had a very different attitude towards learning. It may only need small amounts of money, time and other resources to ensure that the physical spaces where we work with children in church will give these children a sense that they are valued. They will, in turn, respond positively.

Many churches have invested in vastly improved facilities that are used for a range of church activities, including their children's work. This means you may need to compromise on the décor and furnishings – what might be ideal for your fives to nines on a Sunday might be less ideal for the women's prayer meeting on Wednesday – although the differences in requirements may be less than you first think, and it may be that everyone finds those orange plastic chairs, which were bought back in the 1970s, really uncomfortable! If you don't meet in your own building, the decoration will largely be beyond your control. But even then you can put up posters and the children's artwork, remembering to display them at child-eye height, and not your own.

If you have to be responsible for switching on the heating in your venue, make sure that you or another adult arrives early enough to ensure that the room is warm when the children arrive. Look at your lighting options. If children prefer lower lighting levels, is there sufficient light from windows to avoid needing to switch the venue lights on? Or can you just have some lights on? If you can have them on at one end of the hall, but not the other, consider moving the children towards the darker end. You may need to sit yourself directly below one of the lights that is switched on, as your own requirement is likely to be for a higher lighting level. Argue with the church treasurer, if necessary, that you are saving on the lighting bill so that you can spend more on the heating (not strictly true, of course, but it will be a good discussion opener!).

Can you be more creative in your room layout, and give the children the option of not sitting on chairs in rows or round a table? A range of low, comfortable chairs, bean-bags and cushions would be ideal, but you could sit on the floor. If you don't have a carpet, consider investing in some cheap carpet tiles – or make some from an old carpet that a church member may be discarding. Each child can then have their own square, and sit or sprawl on it as they please. You might just sit on the floor for storytelling or a discussion time, but some writing activities could also be done this way, by providing the children with clipboards to lean on. Other crafts and activities are much easier done at a table, and going from the floor to the table gives the children an opportunity to get up and move. If you don't have tables and chairs that are tailored to the size of the children, and even if you do, some children will be happier standing at the table rather than sitting – again, it enables them to move around.

Unless your room is well away from all the others, you are unlikely to be popular with the rest of your church if you have loud music playing throughout your session time, but you could consider having a CD of favourite songs playing quietly when the children are doing activi-ties that don't require talking. Older children in the age range may be becoming self-conscious about singing, and might refuse to participate in an organised time of praise.

If you have music playing, which they have not been asked to sing along with, you may find they learn more effectively, and voluntarily join in with the song! Let the children talk, even about unrelated issues, while they are working alone or in small groups, as long as it does not distract either others or themselves from the task.

Spending some time thinking about your teaching area, before you even start thinking about the content of your teaching, can pay dividends. If the children feel comfortable, they will be more receptive to the lesson, and are far less likely to be disruptive or distracting.

Your church

While the layout, decoration, lighting and temperature of the room you meet in will impact on the way children receive your teaching, what they learn will also be affected by the people around them – and not just their teachers. All your church members are part of the environment in which you meet.

Five- to nine-year-olds want to belong. They need to hear and experience the stories, beliefs and observances of their church community. These are not just stories from the Bible and stories of faithful people from history or today; they include the stories of key events in your church year, and the stories of your members that the children will pick up at coffee time or listening to family chatter at home. What is the attitude of your older members towards the children – those in leadership and everyone else? Are children accepted, included and welcomed, or are they seen as a barely tolerated nuisance, refusing to sit still and making a noise at inappropriate times? It is a huge responsibility and quite frightening to consider, but the way the adults from your church behave, both among themselves in and out of the church environment, and towards the children, will have as big an influence on children's faith development as the Bible stories they are taught.

The children need to feel they have something to contribute. How are they represented on your PCC or leadership group? Does someone have the responsibility to think about the impact of every church decision on the children? Rather than asking the question, 'How can we keep the children occupied while the grown-ups do this project?' do you ask, 'What can the children contribute to this project?' Children can be involved in prayer events, fund-raising events, missionary support by sending emails and pictures, preparation for all-age services, preparation for other all-age events, and many other aspects of church life. Every time their opinion is sought or their help is requested, they are further integrated into their faith community. This is a significant way of helping spiritual development, and is an important complement to the Bible learning and life application discussions that will take place in more formal sessions. Every time you affirm children's contributions, their sense of self-worth is enhanced. Every time you ignore or overlook them, they are made to feel inferior compared to the other members (adults) within the community.

Involving children in church life, and seeking to ensure that you are providing them with excellent sessions, will also minimise any disruption caused by bored children.

4. A Pattern for Learning

The learning cycle

For all of us, effective learning follows a cycle. We will never learn something thoroughly unless we can see the point of the information. Supposing you have always bought cakes from an excellent baker, but he has recently closed down and you don't like the ones on sale in the supermarket. Friends are coming for tea on Saturday, and you would really like to have a cake to offer them. You remember the book of cake recipes that you were given for your birthday a few years ago, but have never opened, and go and find it on the bookshelf. Now you can see the value of the book, and you look up the ingredients for a sponge cake and read the method. It sounds easy enough, but you don't feel confident enough to wait until Saturday to make your first ever sponge cake – you collect the ingredients together and follow the recipe carefully. Reassured that you know what to do, you make the cake again on Saturday, and for several other occasions, each time feeling more confident and beginning to remember the quantities and method with a decreasing reliance on the book. Eventually, you decide that you want a change from a plain sponge, and return to the recipe book to discover how to make a chocolate gateau – you are beginning to move around the learning cycle again.

The learning cycle can begin when there is a real-life connection with the lesson to be learned. It may not be that we always start with an awareness of our need to learn – the skill of the teacher in the first part of a lesson is to bring the children to a point where they are thinking, 'This topic sounds interesting, and I'm willing to learn what you want to teach me.' Conversation is often the most effective way of conducting this part of the lesson, possibly sparked by a game or activity, giving children the chance to relate their own experiences – actual or observed – to the focus of the lesson. The next part of the lesson is its heart, the new information to be taught. If your lessons are based on biblical principles, this is where you will introduce the children to a Bible story. Working with five- to nine-year-olds, you will generally be teaching them a new story, although occasionally you will be bringing new insights to an already known text. Once you have told the story in an appropriate way, then you will need to ask questions to confirm that the children have understood – it is easy to assume, mistakenly, that the children have correctly heard the story you think you have told! The third step of the learning cycle is to practise the information, to explore the Bible story, and to begin to understand its relevance for today. Learning a story is not the same as practising cake-making, and can take a variety of forms. Drama, art, crafts, games, quizzes and writing activities can all play a role, and will be more or less effective, depending on the child's learning preferences. The final part of the cycle is to make the lesson focus, the teaching point drawn out from the story, applicable to each individual child. The teacher needs to know how the children can be expected to apply the lesson, but needs to be flexible enough to accommodate children wishing to add their own ideas.

As we explore the learning cycle, it becomes apparent that children with different learning styles and preferences will perform better, and want to assume a more active role, at different stages of the lesson. Imaginative learners, who enjoy talking and sharing their ideas, will be happy to participate at the start of the cycle, helping everyone to understand how the lesson focus fits in with their own experiences. The analytic learners come to the fore in the second stage of the cycle. They will not have contributed much in the first stage, always reluctant to speak, in case they are seen as missing the point. However, they will show an enthusiasm for learning the story, and will ask questions that help the rest of the group build an understanding of its meaning that wouldn't otherwise occur. Without the analytic learner's rigour at this stage, the rest of the group would be too anxious to push on and would miss learning important facts. The common-sense learners will particularly enjoy the third stage of the cycle, and they will encourage the whole group to spend time exploring and reinforcing the learning in a variety of ways. They will follow the instructions for an activity once, and will then ask what happens if you change the rules and do it a different way. This way, they will bring added dimensions to the lesson. Finally, the dynamic learners will make the group address the question, 'What are we going to do about this?' They will often come up with a series of crazy and totally impractical ideas, but there will be times when they find wonderfully creative ways of putting faith into action that even take their teacher by surprise.

Although everyone will have a place in the learning cycle where they perform at their best, it is still essential for each of us to follow the whole cycle through to learn effectively. In a group setting, children who experience the complete learning cycle every lesson will know that they always get an opportunity within each session to perform in the way they like best, and that will begin to give them the confidence to try new things that fall outside their main areas of strength. But we also know that each of us, as teachers, have one or two preferred teaching styles that will match particular segments of the learning cycle. If time is short, we will always tend to stress those parts of the cycle, cutting short the rest because they seem less important to us. If we don't want to exclude some of our children from developing to their full potential, then we must practise giving equal weight to every part of the lesson.

Now all of our five children can be given the opportunity to learn effectively. Serena and Tom will particularly enjoy the first part of the session, chatting about their own experiences and allowing the others to think about the lesson focus in a concrete way. Josh will contribute if he can tell a story about his family; Tom may talk to one of the other boys rather than the group, and Melissa will probably remain quiet. Melissa will be the one that most enjoys the story time. She will answer the review questions, as long as she is sure she knows the answer. Natalie would prefer to act out the story, and the others will begin to fidget if they are not given the opportunity to move around as they review the story or learn the Bible verse. A range of activities will enable the children to explore and reinforce the session focus. Melissa, Tom and Serena will enjoy musical activities; Natalie will particularly enjoy role-play; Tom and Josh will enjoy active games – as will Natalie, if she is a team leader. Melissa will prefer sitting at the table, writing, painting, doing crafts and completing activity sheets. Natalie may join in the art and craft activities, as long as they are not too complex, and Josh will also take part in the crafts – but he'd prefer to sit on the floor than at the table! Natalie will be the one that gets carried away with ideas in the final stage of the session. She will try to persuade everyone else to get involved in a scheme to show their response to the session.

The learning cycle

- Begin with what you already know.
- Learn something new.
- Practise this new knowledge.
- Creatively apply your new knowledge.

You now have new knowledge, on which you can build by going round the cycle again.

The Master Practitioner

Some excellent demonstrations of the effectiveness of the learning cycle are found in the Gospels. Jesus was the master teacher, and the master storyteller. He knew that he had to capture the attention and interest of his audience, be it one or thousands, before he told them a story. He then would lead them through the story, making sure they had understood, before showing them what his teachings meant to them personally.

His parables were stories which captured the attention of the listener by relating to a topic about which they were familiar and interested – increasing yields by planting on the best soil, caring for flocks of sheep, searching for missing treasure, being forgiven for debts owed, etc. Once Jesus had told his story – always short, for maximum attention – he would ask questions, to involve his listeners and help them come to a new and deeper understanding of his teaching. Then they could be challenged to see the application to their own lives.

Just one example of Jesus' teaching is the incident where he met the Samaritan woman at the well (John 4:6–39).

> Jesus, tired as he was from the journey, sat down by the well. It was about the sixth hour.
>
> When a Samaritan woman came to draw water, Jesus said to her, 'Will you give me a drink?'
>
> . . . 'How can you ask me for a drink?' (For Jews do not associate with Samaritans.)
>
> Jesus answered her, 'If you knew the gift of God and who it is that asks you for a drink, you would have asked him and he would have given you living water.'
>
> 'Sir,' the woman said, 'you have nothing to draw with and the well is deep. Where can you get this living water?' (verses 6–11)

The woman had to collect water from the well every day, and because of her marital status, she went at the hottest time of the day, when no one else was around. She wouldn't have expected Jesus to speak to her, let alone offer her a way of apparently never having to carry out this chore of drawing water again. This is the beginning of the learning cycle – the woman understands the purpose of water, and she is interested.

> Jesus answered, 'Everyone who drinks this water will be thirsty again, but whoever drinks the water I give him will never thirst. Indeed, the water I give him will become in him a spring of water welling up to eternal life.' (verses 13–14)

The second step of the learning cycle: Jesus gave the woman information – just one simple, but life-changing, fact.

> The woman said to him, 'Sir, give me this water so that I won't get thirsty and have to keep coming here to draw water.'
>   He told her, 'Go, call your husband and come back.'
>   'I have no husband,' she replied.
>   Jesus said to her, 'You are right when you say you have no husband . . .'
>   'Sir,' the woman said, 'I can see that you are a prophet . . .'
>   Jesus declared, '. . . God is spirit, and his worshippers must worship in spirit and in truth.'
>   The woman said, 'I know that Messiah' (called Christ) 'is coming. When he comes, he will explain everything to us.'
>   Then Jesus declared, 'I who speak to you am he.' (verses 15–26)

The woman needed to make a personal connection with the information she had been given. Jesus gave himself credibility, by demonstrating that he knew facts about her that a stranger couldn't readily know, and then he conversed with her, answering her questions and helping her understand his teaching.

Then, leaving her water jar, the woman went back to the town and said to the people, 'Come, see a man who told me everything I ever did. Could this be the Christ?' They came out of the town and made their way towards him . . . Many of the Samaritans from that town believed in him because of the woman's testimony, 'He told me everything I ever did.' (verses 28–30, 39)

Finally, being sure of her new information, the woman knew exactly what she must do with it – she hurried back to the town and called everyone to come and discover the Christ for themselves. The people knew this woman wouldn't normally draw attention to herself and, because of her testimony, they also believed in Jesus.

5. A Variety of Activities

Stories

Stories are a very powerful way of teaching five- to nine-year-olds. They have a strong desire to belong to family and community, and experience belonging by knowing the stories. These stories can range from the latest events surrounding family members – such as the birth of a cousin – through the traditions and myths of the local community or family – such as the size of the marrow that won the local show in 1975, or the way that the family celebrates birthdays – to the wider known stories of history and faith. Each story helps children understand their community and their place within it.

Stories for five to nines need to be simply constructed with a beginning, a middle and an end. They need to be told in simple language and concentrate on people, objects and events, rather than abstract ideas and concepts. Remember that under sevens have little concept of time or distance and openings such as 'long ago' or 'far away' are sufficient and less distracting than long, introductory paragraphs setting the story in a time or place outside their own experience. However, links to their own understanding are important – telling Bible stories that rely on donkeys and small sailing boats as the only means of travel may need to be preceded by discussion about the various modes of transport available to us today, and how they were not available to Jesus or Paul when they lived long ago.

Visual aids are important when you are telling stories to this age group. Over several sessions, use a variety of aids that will appeal to different learning styles – use pictures, video, objects, drama, puppets or crafts. On occasions, involve the children directly in the storytelling, having them act out or mime parts, either individually, or as a group, or by using interactive crafts. When you have told a story, check that the children have understood it correctly – ask questions either directly, or as a game, or quiz, or through other activities, such as role-play.

How much of the Bible should we teach five to nines?

Much of the Old Testament involves stories of violence but, unlike many of today's films, cartoons and computer games, the stories are not written to focus on the violence, but rather on the eternal truth of obedience and sin. The Old Testament demonstrates God's control over the world and the need to punish disobedience – the story of Noah tells of (a few) people who obeyed being saved on the ark and of the remaining (many) people who did not obey being drowned. God allowed children to suffer the punishment of community disobedience and permitted them to witness violent acts. We should not exclude the Bible stories we tell to this age group solely on the basis of their violence, although it is right to exclude them if their focus is not appropriate to their level of understanding, such as sexual sin. It is important though, to ensure that children are not afraid of God – they need to have stories of Old Testament punishment tempered by teaching about Jesus' kindness. However, passages that teach that Jesus lives in our heart, or that we need to be born again, are concepts which children of this age can't understand. As a concrete fact they know it can't be true, and as abstract teaching they need the idea to be supported with clear explanations about what we really mean and with contemporary examples of the concepts in practice (this is not a bad rule to follow when talking to adults, either).

Children will be particularly interested in stories about characters, especially if there is plenty of action surrounding them. Moses, Joseph, David, Jonah, Esther, Paul and, of course, Jesus are just a few examples. Introduce them to stories that make God's response to prayer very tangible (throughout the story of Moses, there are many examples, particularly the provision of food and water in the desert, Exodus 15:22 – 17:7). Show them concrete examples of the way that people's characters were changed once the Holy Spirit descended upon them (an example is Peter healing the crippled beggar and then having the courage to face the Sanhedrin and declare salvation through Christ, Acts 3:1 – 4:21). Take advantage of the fact that they are hungry for information, and teach them the stories of the Bible writers – Moses and the tablets of stone; Daniel and his visions, which he recorded; Baruch, Jeremiah's scribe; Luke; the writers of the Epistles, and others.

Jesus knew the power of storytelling, and how important it is to ground stories that teach something new in the things that we already understand. The parables of the New Testament relate directly to the experiences of the fishermen and farmers, officials and priests of Israel two thousand years ago. Many of those experiences are unknown to children today, and they can't have the same direct teaching impact. We can relate the parables of Jesus to children as stories; we can also tell new parables, using current-day experiences that teach the same eternal truth, and we can begin to help children understand the application of the story to their own behaviour. Gradually, as children grow from five to nine, they will begin to make their own connection from parable to application.

Around the age of five or six, children are beginning to understand the difference between fact and fantasy, and they will almost certainly be exposed to stories of magical beings and events. At the same time, they will be learning of the certainties of science at school, and so how will they interpret the stories of miracles? We should not impose our own levels of reasoning on children – they transition seamlessly from belief in Father Christmas or the Tooth Fairy into knowing it is a harmless piece of make-believe and, in a similar way their understanding of miracles will mature as they grow older.

For more information on telling stories in appropriate ways for five- to nine-year olds see the *Children's Ministry Guide to Storytelling* (Children's Ministry, 2002). Lynda Neilands' books *50 Five-Minute Stories* (Children's Ministry, 1996), *50 Stories for Special Occasions* (Children's Ministry, 1998) and *50 Life-Building Stories* (Children's Ministry, 2002) are excellent sources of appropriate stories for telling to this age group.

Bible learning

Childhood is a golden age for learning. Children are generally keen to learn and things that we commit to memory as children seem to remain with us long after we have forgotten facts that we learned when we were older. I remember learning a long poem at school when I was about nine years old – 'Off the Ground', by Walter de la Mare. I have never needed to know or recite the poem since, but I can still recall the opening lines:

> Three jolly farmers
> Once bet a pound
> Each dance the other would
> Off the ground.

I have checked, and this is an accurate recollection, after well over thirty years. My memory of the remaining four pages is somewhat hazy, but I can still recite a surprisingly unnecessary amount!

Of course, when I was at school, we learned a great deal more by rote than children do today – French verbs, historical dates, geographical facts, maths formulae, chemical symbols, and much more, were committed to memory and tested. Now it is considered appropriate for children to spend more time learning where to find the information rather than the facts themselves. So should we content ourselves with teaching children to find their way round a Bible and a concordance, rather than encouraging them to memorise Bible verses?

At the age of eleven, I learned about the south-east of England in geography (not the area where I lived at that time). Now that I do live in the dip between the South

Downs and the High Weald, I understand the structure of the chalk escarpments that I drive past every morning, and I know why we get far less rain in our garden than our friends experience in the town three miles up the road. If I hadn't *known* that information, I don't imagine I would have ever thought to look it up, but it does add an extra dimension to living where I do. It's the same with Bible verses: I know that the Lord is 'forgiving and good' (Psalm 86:5); I know I can 'trust in God' (John 14:1). I know these things with certainty because I can quote them from the Bible. Those certainties are in the background of my everyday living, and I don't have to think that they are probably true and wonder whether I ought to start searching through a concordance to check it out.

So, yes, we should help children to memorise Bible verses. However, I don't recommend that you just teach them in isolation. If they relate to the focus of your session, the children will understand the point of learning them. Use as many senses as possible when teaching the verse, to help commit it to memory. Singing or chanting can be more memorable than just reciting, and visual reminders – particularly actions – can be powerful aids to memory. Learning is helped by repetition, and it may be better to take the same verse over a series of sessions, ensuring that after a month the children have all stored it in their long-term memory, rather than teaching several verses, all of which are forgotten.

Puppets and drama

Puppets and drama can be used in a wide variety of ways with children. They can be used as visual aids, with the children as observers, or they can be used as reinforcing activities, where children can be involved in making puppets, inventing dialogue and manipulating the puppets, or acting out the drama.

Puppets can say things that children dare not. They can dialogue with children and elicit responses that the children may be too reticent to voice in conversation with adults. They can be made of wooden spoons or paper plates, be hand puppets or sophisticated muppet-style puppets. They can represent children, or Bible characters, or be blue, hairy, fantasy creatures. They can whisper to you; you can openly speak their lines; you can be a ventriloquist, or speak from behind a screen, or they can mime to music.

You can use drama or puppets at every stage of the learning cycle. Actors or puppets, having a conversation in a setting that would be familiar to children, can stimulate an opening discussion. You can use a puppet or an actor dressed as a character from the story to narrate a Bible passage or, alternatively, several actors or puppets can perform the entire story. Drama is a particularly strong way of bringing Bible parables up-to-date. After the telling of a Bible story, children could use simple stick puppets or role-play to retell it to each other. Role-play is also a very effective way of involving children in working through possible ways they can put Bible teaching into effect in their everyday lives at school and home.

Puppets can also be used to involve children in worship, particularly as a visual aid accompanying a song. I have seen this work to tremendous effect after a lively time of dancing praise when a single puppet, miming to a CD, brought about two hundred children to focus quietly on a song of love for Jesus.

Games

Games can be used to introduce a session, to check for understanding, and to generally reinforce learning in an active way. Some games and activities will take place sitting down. Secular, shop-bought games, such as Happy Family cards or Mastermind, can be used to start a discussion about families, or to demonstrate the need to be patient when trying to work out what God wants us to do. You can buy, or make your own, board-games or puzzles that will help retell a Bible story. A quiz about Jonah could be scored by colouring part of a fish each time the children answer a question correctly, or a quiz could be based on picture clues on an OHP or flip chart.

Other games and activities can be much more active. Relay races on a theme relating to the session will be popular with older children in the age group. Games where children change places, with a catcher trying to intercept, according to a characteristic or a predetermined name, or hunting games can also be used to introduce a topic. Quizzes can be made very active. True/false questions, where children have to run to different parts of the room to indicate their answer, help release pent-up energy, and human noughts and crosses brings an interesting twist to the scoring of a team quiz.

At five years old, children still find it hard to lose, and are only just beginning to work with others, so twos and threes work better than large groups, and adult support is still important. Choose games and activities that involve everyone for most of the time, such as Follow the Leader, or hunting objects that tell the story, or quizzes, where everyone can participate by showing their answer (maybe holding up different coloured or shaped signs to represent 'yes' or 'no'). By the age of seven or eight, children will enjoy working as a team, have a desire to win, which means they are also learning to accept defeat, and have the self-discipline to wait for their turn. Relay race games, team quizzes and charades will be popular.

For more ideas, check out *100 Children's Club Activities*, by Jan Dyer (Children's Ministry, 2001).

Art and craft

Craft or art activities can be used in a variety of ways throughout the learning cycle. As children arrive, they can join in an art or craft activity that is then used to introduce a session theme. Old magazines and newspapers can be looked through to find pictures of families that can be stuck onto frieze paper and used to introduce a story on the importance of family. Handprints can be a good way of introducing a topic on being helpful. Making simple boats can start a conversation that discovers what the children know about boats and sailing and then leads into a story about Paul's missionary travels.

Crafts, which either the teacher or the children have made, can be used as interactive visual aids during the story time. The boats made at the beginning of the lesson about Paul can be used in the story to act out a storm, or Paul travelling from one town to another. Children can make happy/sad puppets, drawing faces on either side of a paper plate, that enable them to join in telling a story, identifying a character's changing emotions. Or more complex crafts, such as a story wheel that reveals seven different pictures showing the creation story, can be made by the teacher in advance – or possibly by children at the older end of the range, as a review activity.

Illustration, using pencils, paints or collage materials is another good way to reinforce a story and check that the children have understood it. Always let children illustrate in their own way – the art or craft is part of their learning experience, and the finished product is not generally important – and while they are working, you can take the opportunity to talk to them one-on-one, or in small groups. Younger children generally draw from experience rather than imagination, so don't insist they paint a picture of an angel if they tell you they can't because they have never seen one.

Beyond checking for understanding, crafts can be used to provide the children with ways of taking a lesson home with them – either as an aid to remember the story and retell it to family and friends, or as a reminder of the application. Simple character puppets, a picture with a moving part (such as the stone in front of the tomb that can be rolled aside), or a storybook can act as story reminders. Mobiles, shaped bookmarks or prayer aids are all possible examples of crafts that will remind the children of the lesson learned once they are at home.

Art and craft can also be used to enhance worship with children – a cube could have six different ideas for prayer topics on each face; paintings, banners, or flags could be made that illustrate songs or themes; a psalm could be illustrated and shown as the passage is read.

For more ideas, check out *100 Simple Bible Craft Ideas for Children*, by Sue Price (Children's Ministry, 1998).

Music and rhyme

Rhyme and rhythms are excellent ways of helping children learn. By the age of five, most children will be able to sing reasonably in tune, and will be beginning to be able to keep a rhythm going on a percussion instrument. However, if you are using music and rhyme as a teaching tool, it is most effective when you keep the tune and the words simple.

Look for poems in children's anthologies that will introduce a topic. Sing simple action songs that retell a Bible story, or relate to the life application. There are lots of tapes and CDs of children's songs, some of which are specific to Bible passages or memory verses, and which often come with backing tracks so, if you don't have musicians in your group, you can still sing along. And if you can't find something that is already published, write a rhyme or new words to an existing tune yourself.

Children can have fun writing their own poems and even raps, which they may like to perform to each other, or even a wider audience. They can also make percussion instruments – the home-made variety will often be quieter than the real thing, which may be seen as an added bonus! Working out a rhythm for a Bible verse can be a different way to help children learn the words.

For more ideas, check out *50 Musical Activities for Children*, by Alison Hedger (Children's Ministry, 2001).

6. The Learning Cycle in Action

This chapter provides three specific examples of session outlines that show the learning cycle being applied for teaching in a variety of situations. Whenever you are planning, you must take account of helper to child ratio recommendations and other health, safety and Children Act requirements. You will find these issues addressed in another book within the series of *Children's Ministry Guides*.

A Bible teaching session for 5–7s

This example session takes the story of Paul and Barnabas healing a lame man in the power of the Holy Spirit (Acts 14:6–18). It draws out, as its focus, the fact that God will give us the power to do his work.

Grab attention by having a range of items that need batteries to work (torch, clock, radio, personal stereo, toy, hand-held computer game . . .) that have had the batteries removed. As the children arrive, they can examine the items. Start the session by selecting different children or helpers to describe each item. Point out that none of them are working – ask what they need to make them function. Produce the batteries and make the items work – batteries produce power that makes things work. List items that the children can think of that need electricity to make them work.

Explain that the Bible story shows God's power. God's power isn't electricity, which can hurt us; it's power given through the Holy Spirit. At the right time in the story, have two helpers carry a third (the lame man) through the 'crowd' of children to listen to Paul and Barnabas. Have pictures of Paul and Barnabas to show as you tell the Bible story in age-appropriate language. After the story, ask everyone to sit in a circle, on the floor, with their outstretched legs pointing inwards. Encourage the children to feel their legs – the bones, the muscles and the tendons. Explain that we need to use the muscles or else they waste away and won't work. If we hurt our legs, we have to do exercises to get them to work properly again. The lame man in the story had never walked – he wouldn't have known he should do exercises to stop his muscles wasting. When he tried to stand up, his leg muscles should not have supported him. God's power made him well and made his muscles strong, too. Help the children remember with a rhyme that they can act out:

> Not a shake and not a wobble,
> Not a stumble, not a hobble.
> Up he jumped with no delay,
> 'God's power has made me well today!'

Introduce a memory verse from the Bible: 'Great is our Lord and mighty in power' (Psalm 147:5).

Divide the children into two lines facing each other. One line stamps their feet and shouts, 'Great is our Lord.' The other line stamps and shouts in reply, 'and mighty in power'. Both lines shout, 'Psalm one, forty-seven, verse five.' After several repetitions, change round, so that all the children learn both parts.

Reinforce the learning with a range of activities that can be done by all children sequentially, or can be offered simultaneously, each run by a different helper, allowing the children to choose:

- Have several cards with actions on – hop, jump, bunny hop, spin round, jumping jacks . . . Put the children in pairs and let each pair choose a card. They must see how many of their actions they can do in one minute. (The lame man had never been able to do any of these things. God changed his life on the outside and on the inside.)

- Have two square pictures – about 10 cm x 10 cm – of the lame man before and after he is healed. Cut each picture into four vertical strips. Reassemble the two pictures as one, alternating strips from the two pictures. Photocopy the new single picture, one for each child. They can 'concertina fold' on the lines that mark the strips. Stand the picture on a table. View from one side to see the lame man. View from the other side to see him healed. (Story reminder.)

- Have a series of pictures showing different Bible stories from Acts that show when God's power helped Paul. Let the children match the pictures to statements, such as God's power helped Paul to make sick people well, God's power helped Paul to tell other people about Jesus . . . Also have a series of pictures that show children in appropriate situations that match to corresponding statements: God's power helps us to pray for sick people to get well, God's power helps us to tell our friends about Jesus . . . (God helped Paul in many ways and he will still help us in the same ways today.)

• Make up actions to a song on the theme. (Reinforces the session focus.)

Help the children apply the Bible, learning by explaining that Paul and Barnabas were given power from God to help them tell and show lots of people the good news about Jesus. He wants people today, whose lives have been changed by his power, to work for him and tell others about Jesus. If possible, bring a couple of adults known to the children to explain simply what they do in God's power. Hand out a variety of objects – hard hat, nurse's cap, policeman's helmet, supermarket bag, briefcase, school bag, butcher's apron – one for each child. Lead a time of prayer, by inviting God to change the life of each child, giving them the power of the Holy Spirit. Thank God for giving us the power to work for him wherever we live or work. Invite each child to thank God that we can work for him if we are a . . . (describe the occupation of the person represented by their object).

Of our children, Serena, Josh and Natalie (as five to sevens) may have participated in this session. Josh would have enjoyed the opening activity, with the battery-operated items, and Serena would have been keen to share her knowledge about her tape player needing electricity to work. All of them would have enjoyed the game – Natalie would have insisted on pretending she was a cow and made all the right noises as she tried to escape from the field! Serena and Josh would have particularly enjoyed finding out about their leg muscles and bones and Natalie would have overacted the action rhyme, making everyone laugh again. If they could only choose one activity, Serena would make up actions to the song, Josh would work with a partner to see how many of the actions they could do in a minute, and Natalie would choose the activity of matching the pictures of Paul and modern children with the statements. She would come up with an idea about putting on a drama about Paul at school to tell everyone else about God's power and would also ask to help lead the prayer time.

Note:

This session is based on session 3 of the Choosing God's Way unit from the Children's Ministry Teaching Programme, KidZone Blue/Gold Leader's Guide (originally available from Summer 2000 while stocks last, and due to be reissued in Summer 2004).

A holiday club session for 7–9's

A holiday club session will differ from a Bible teaching session, in that it will generally be one of a series of closely linked sessions over several days; it will usually be longer, and it will often have a majority of non-church-linked children. However, the principles of the learning cycle still apply. The children need to become *engaged with the topic*; they need to *hear the story*; they need to have the opportunity to *explore its meaning*, and they need to be encouraged to think how the teaching will have an *impact on their lives*.

Holiday clubs will typically last for a couple of hours in the morning. In some cases, it will have an afternoon session as well, and in such instances the afternoon should be more fun activities than learning, and be an opportunity to include some more time-consuming activities that would typically fall into the third stage of the learning cycle. The final step of the learning cycle can then be placed either at the end of the morning session or at the end of the day.

This example is a session that is one (probably the fourth of five) from a series based on the story of Noah. It takes as its focus 'God wants me to trust him' and studies the Bible passage from the time that the flood waters started to recede until Noah, his family and all the animals disembarked: Genesis 8:1–19.

Start the session with a game that will involve some of the children actively and capture everyone's attention. Set an obstacle course and at its end place a bowl with a thick mixture of flour and water containing a key. Have your main session leaders dressed as Mr and Mrs Noah. Mr Noah, blindfolded, says that he has lost the key to the lion's cage and needs to find it, but he can't see where he is going. Mrs Noah offers to help by leading him. 'Trust me,' she says. She then leads him through the obstacle course to the bowl and guides his hands into the gloopy mixture. Invite a few children to be led through the course, changing it slightly each time after blindfolding them, and adding elements, such as walking across crunchy cereal and crawling under a table hanging with lengths of wool (elements which, although not difficult, will cause someone who is blindfolded to experience the unexpected).

Mr and Mrs Noah can lead a discussion on the meaning of trust and who we can trust to help us (ultimately, God is the only one we can trust completely). Then, move to a time of singing – the 'Arky, Arky' song will probably be a theme song for the series, but there are others on the theme of trust that can be introduced.

Remind the children of the story so far, and introduce today's story: Noah trusted God to bring him and his family safely out of the ark when the flood was finally over. It wasn't easy to wait, but Noah continued to trust God. Move to sit in or round the large ark that the children have constructed in earlier sessions, and Mr and Mrs Noah can tell the Bible story – have visual aids, or even helpers dressed as the dove and the raven to come and tell their part in the story.

Add a memory verse at this point – 'I trust in God's unfailing love for ever and ever' (Psalm 52:8). In advance of the session, write each word on a separate sheet of paper and tape each sheet under a different chair. Ask the children to feel under their seats; invite each child with a word to the front, and help them to arrange themselves in the correct order. Everyone can read out the verse, first quietly, then normally and then shouting. Choose children to sit down two by two (just as the animals came out of the ark), repeating the verse in between each pair. When everyone is seated, say the verse again three times – quietly, normally and shouting.

By now it is time for a break – squash (tropical fruit) and a biscuit (animal-shaped and covered in chocolate). After the break, you will need to recapture attention and refocus on the session theme. Play a clip from the Disney *Jungle Book* video – showing Mowgli being enticed by the snake, Kaa, singing the song, 'Trust in me'. Afterwards, ask the children why Mowgli would be wrong to trust Kaa. Remind them that we can always trust God.

Move onto the reinforcing activities – which you may do with everyone participating in one activity at a time, or you may offer at different activity stations, so that children can rotate and assigned leaders can work with smaller groups. The number of activities will depend on your facilities and, especially, the time you have. This segment of the session may last half an hour, or it may cross over into the afternoon and last two or three hours. Offer a variety of games, crafts and paper-based activities that will suit the different learning preferences of all the children you have attending.

Optional activities can include:

- Obstacle course – let all the children have a go at completing the introductory course, in pairs, with one blindfolded. (Sometimes we can't do things by ourselves; we need to trust others to help. We can always trust God.)

- Flood the mud! – find a suitable patch of ground outside for the children to try and flood with cups of water. Let them see how the water drains away when you stop pouring. (God sent a huge flood over the whole earth. When the rains stopped, the water drained away, but it took a long time.)

- Video watch – show the relevant section of a Bible story video. (Story review.)

- Leaves and trees – go outside and use wax crayons to make bark and leaf rubbings; inside, cut cauliflowers with flat cross-sections to make tree prints; grow trees by dropping a blob of runny paint at the bottom of a sheet of paper and using a straw to blow the paint in various directions, making a trunk with branches. (Once the floodwaters subsided, God restored the trees and plants that we need to live.)

- Raven and dove bookmark – have a template of a bird that can be cut out and coloured black on one side, for the raven, and left white on the other, for the dove. The memory verse can be written on the white side. (Story and memory verse reminder.)

- For ever circle – cut strips of paper 2 cm wide and about 30 cm long. Along the full length of one side, write: 'I trust in God's unfailing love'. Turn the strip over and, starting to write at the same end as you started to write 'I . . .', write 'for ever and ever. Psalm 52:8'. Make one twist in the strip, and stick the ends together. Read round the strip – it never comes to an end. (Memory verse and session focus reminder.)

- 'I can always trust God' booklet – fold two sheets of paper together to make an eight-page booklet. On the cover page, write: '(name) can always trust God'. At the top of each of the remaining sheets write a day of the week and: 'I can trust God today to . . .' Leave the rest of the page blank, to fill in during the week.

- Chocolate leaves – paint melted chocolate over mint leaves. Set in a fridge or freezer before peeling off the leaves.

- Man the lifeboats – assign different parts of a ship to the playing area. Players move around the area, running to the parts of the ship called by a leader. When the leader calls, 'Man the lifeboats!' everyone runs to the assigned area and the last to arrive is out, presumed drowned. (Fun, but on topic game to use up energy.)

After the activity time, gather the children into small groups, each with a leader. Help the children think of times when they might need to trust God. Either pray in groups or let the children pray silently while a song plays in the background. Finally, Mr and Mrs Noah introduce another time of singing and then close the session by reinforcing the session focus and leading the children in reciting the memory verse three times again (quietly, normally and shouting). Encourage the children to take home their raven and dove bookmark and/or their for ever circle to remind them that they can always trust God.

Of our children, Natalie, Tom and Melissa (as sevens and over) may have attended the holiday club. Tom would have been keen to have a go on the obstacle course, while Melissa would have declined if invited, but she would have been able to answer any questions the leaders asked about the story so far. She would hope that none of the memory verse words were under her chair, whereas Natalie and Tom would be excited if they found a word. Tom would wriggle through the video, looking forward to the games and activities that were coming up. Melissa would prefer that the video lasted for the rest of the session, and would be pleased to discover that another video was included in the optional activities. She would choose that, the for ever circle and the booklet as her three choices. Tom would select the obstacle course, man the lifeboats and flood the mud! and Natalie would also choose the obstacle course, along with the chocolate leaves, and the leaves and trees activity. She would be disappointed that there was no drama today, but she would enjoy the opportunity to pray in a small group and would have several suggestions about when she might need to trust God, as would Tom. Melissa would listen to the others' suggestions and prayers.

Note:

This session is based on session 4 of the Noah material from the Children's Ministry Teaching Programme, KidZone Blue/Gold Leader's Guide.

A kidz klub style meeting for 5–9s

Some churches now prefer to have front-led meetings for a large number of children spanning a wide age range. With a gifted leader, these meetings can often be very effective for evangelising non-church-based children. They are less appropriate for discipling children who are church regulars, as they do not allow leaders to develop a close relationship with a small group of children. Smaller groups allow the leaders to shape sessions that reflect the particular stages the children are at on their pathway of faith development. However, front-led meetings can still effectively follow the learning cycle.

This session is based on the story of Joseph being reunited with his brothers (Genesis 42–47). It takes as its focus the desire that God has for us to do good to others.

As children arrive, ask for their help in setting out your venue. Be very clear in saying how much you appreciate their help and how pleased you are that they have come along. Have helpers act out three situations:

• Two children, James and Sean, had been best friends for a long time. Sean has now become friendly with an older boy. He tells James that he is too babyish. James is upset. After a short time, Sean's new friend gets fed up with Sean. Sean wants to be friends with James again.

- One night, Catherine's older sister hides under Catherine's bed. Catherine gets into bed and is almost asleep when she hears a scary, moaning sound. Catherine is really frightened and starts to cry. Catherine's sister starts to laugh, and when Catherine realises it is a trick she gets very angry.
- Trina's little brother has taken her collection of special stones and buried them in the garden. Now he says he can't remember where they are, and Trina is really mad. Trina's mum asks Trina to keep an eye on her brother while she pops next door. Trina's brother locks himself in the garden shed, and can't turn the key to get out.

Ask for ideas as to what James, Catherine and Trina should do.

Introduce the Bible story by pointing out that when people are mean to us we often want to get our own back. It is much harder to continue to be kind and friendly to those people. The Bible story is about someone who had to decide whether to get his own back or whether to do good.

Set up a throne for a leader to sit on, acting out the part of Joseph. Have puppets to play his brothers. Let Joseph give a very brief résumé of his story – stressing how unkind his brothers had been to him. Joseph continues to tell his story, with the puppets acting out and speaking the parts of the brothers. Give every child a few sheets of newspaper, and show them how to make a palm tree, rolling the sheets into a tube and tucking the bottom inside to keep it from unrolling. Then make four tears, about 15 cms long, downwards from the top of the tube. Fold the 'leaves' downwards over the 'trunk'. Mark out an area of 'desert' on the stage, using sand. Divide the group into two or more teams, and allocate an area of desert to each team. Have a quiz that includes questions checking for an understanding of the story. Anyone who correctly answers a question can come and plant their palm tree in their team's area of the desert. The team with the most trees wins.

Select twelve children to be Joseph and his brothers. Give each a tea towel head-dress which has one word of the Bible verse or its reference pinned to the back: 'Do not be overcome by evil, but overcome evil with good' (Romans 12:21). Stand all twelve children in order, with their backs to the rest, so that the verse can be read out. After a few repetitions, turn one child round. Repeat until the children can recite the verse without prompts.

Divide the children into smaller groups for a craft and activity time.

- Make origami bread baskets.
- Use reference books to research the process of making bread from the time that grain seed is first planted. Illustrate this process on a large frieze, using paints and collage materials, such as grains, flour, and flat breads.
- Paint the words of the Bible verse on stones. Arrange them around an oasis made in each team's desert area, using a small bowl of water and the newspaper palm trees, painted with thick green and brown paints.

Bring the children back into the large group and have a time of singing. Produce a large origami bread basket, with a selection of real breads and several card loaf shapes. Talk about how God wants us to do good, rather than get our own back, when people are unkind to us. Brainstorm examples. Write the children's ideas on the card loaves, and fix them to a display panel. Use the ideas as a basis for prayer.

With this session you may need to be prepared for children to share incidents of adults being unkind through abuse, and you should ensure that all your helpers are aware of your church policy for dealing with such revelations.

All of our children could have attended this session. With the exception of Melissa, they would all find it a long time to sit through the role-play and Bible story, although the puppets would capture the attention of Serena, Josh and Natalie. Tom would get told off for wriggling in his seat and turning to talk to the boy next to him, and Natalie would wish she could have been involved in the drama. The four younger children will hope they get chosen to answer a question so they can get up with their palm tree. Melissa will know the answers to the quiz questions, but will whisper them to someone else on her team rather than be embarrassed by having to go out in front of all the other children. Serena, Natalie and Tom will choose to create the oasis. Josh will select the bread basket activity, and Melissa will be really interested in the bread-making process activity. They will all join in with the singing, but Serena and the boys will be itching to run around outside as soon as the session is over.

Note:

This session is based on session 12 of the Choosing God's Way unit from the Children's Ministry Teaching Programme, KidZone Blue/Gold Leader's Guide (originally available from Summer 2000 while stocks last and due to be reissued in Summer 2004).

Moving forward

The preceding three sections show very specific programme outlines, but they act to demonstrate the learning cycle in action and give examples of activities that are appropriate for children in the five- to nine-year-old age range.

I hope, by now, you will feel that you know at least a little more about the children that you work with. As you have considered the typical developmental characteristics of children, you will have compared those you know against these averages. Some children will be a close match, at least in some areas, while others will be quite different. If you use published materials for your children's work, remember that the authors cannot know the individuals you have in your groups, and can only write for the typical child. You may need to adapt for children with reading difficulties, children who are particularly able at thinking in abstract ways, or children with specific special needs.

The chapter on learning preferences may have thrown light on the reason that children you know behave in certain ways. Alternatively, or additionally, it may have helped you understand why you adopt the teaching style you do, and why some children seem to receive your sessions so much more positively than others. Some published materials clearly apply the learning cycle, and so it is possible to ensure that you select resources that provide sessions structured to take the learning preferences of all the children you teach into account.

Whatever your situation, this book will have achieved its aim if it helps you with practical understanding and new ideas that improve the opportunity for every child you work with to develop a personal relationship with Christ.

Appendix

Discussion Topics

Use these questions on your own, with a colleague, or during a children's workers' team meeting to stimulate discussion or consideration of how you can tailor your sessions more effectively for the five- to nine-year-olds that you work with.

1. Describe the physical, mental, social, emotional, spiritual and faith characteristics of four children that you work with in a similar style to the descriptions of the five children in chapter 1.
2. Assess your own learning preferences – sensory, environmental and style (or work as a pair with someone you know well, and assess each other's preferences). Identify the parts of the learning cycle that you least enjoy teaching, and plan a session that really stresses those steps.
3. Draw a plan of a room that would be the ideal environment and layout for the group you teach. Using that as a guide, decide to make two changes to the layout of the space that you do use.

4. How can you make all the adults in your church more aware of the indirect influence they have on the faith development of the children? Come up with two ideas that you could suggest to the church leadership which would integrate the children more closely into the church community.

Children's Ministry Teaching Programme

- Do you want to see children develop a personal relationship with Jesus?

- Do you want teaching sessions that are fun, biblical, evangelical and interactive?

- Would you like children to enjoy age-appropriate activities as they learn about God?

If you've said YES to any of these questions, you need the Children's Ministry Teaching Programme.

The Children's Ministry Teaching Programme provides four leader's guides covering ages from under 3 to 13+; KidZone activity books for children aged 5-7, 7-9 and 9-11; MiniKidz and KidZone craft books for children aged 3-5 and 5-9, a magazine for those over 11; a CD of music and stories; and FamilyZone with song words, ideas for all-age worship and parents' letters.

**For more information visit our web site
www.childrensministry.co.uk**

CHILDREN'S MINISTRY
Resources

ENHANCING YOUR MINISTRY WITH CHILDREN